Optimist *plays*

THE SONNETEER

Optimist

THE SONNETEER

Optimist *plays*

ISBN 979-8-88722-020-8

Optimist Books by Optimist Creations

optimistcreations.com

THE SONNETEER

An earlier and shorter version of this play was first performed
at Greenside Nicholson Square
as part of the Edinburgh Festival Fringe 2014,
with the cast as follows:

Will / Lecturer – Sebastian Michael
Henry / Student – Tom Medcalf

Directed by Ros Philips

THE SONNETEER

A Play on Passion, Power and Possession
by

Sebastian Michael

with Sonnets by
William Shakespeare

characters

will, m, about 30 – william shakespeare
michael, m, about 50 – a 21st century academic & lecturer

henry, m, about 20 – henry wriothesley,
            the 3rd earl of southampton
tom, m, about 22 – a 21st century student

*the play can be performed as a two-hander with two actors
playing both the historical and contemporary characters, or with
four actors, one pair playing present day michael and tom, and
the other pair playing will and henry respectively.*

*the action moves seamlessly between the present and the past,
at times overlapping; it covers a period of just over three years
from late spring / early summer 1593 to august 1596, and the
approximate equivalent in the present day.*

*blank lines signal thought, action or reaction: nonverbal
communication.*

*where stage directions are given, they are principally there to
make it clear what is supposed to be happening in the play. once
that purpose is fulfilled, they can mostly be ignored: you'll find
your own way of making this work.*

*where characters' names appear in **bold**, this is purely to alert you
to the fact that we're switching from one time frame to another
within a scene – there is no other significance to it.*

*"If a man should importune me to give a reason why I loved him,
I find it could no otherwise be expressed than by making answer:
because it was he, because it was I."*

– Michel de Montaigne (1533-1592)

1

lecture theatre | at will's in london
late spring to early summer: the present | 1593

*[michael on stage, as he reaches the end of his lecture; tom in the
audience]*

michael   and so to conclude
               ladies and gentlemen:
               everything
               is conjecture
               except
               the words

*[lunges forward, speaks directly to a member of the audience;
then another, then another]*

> *Shall I compare thee to a summer's day?*
> *Thou art more lovely and more temperate:*
> *Rough winds do shake the darling buds of May,*
> *And summer's lease hath all too short a date:*
> *Sometime too hot the eye of heaven shines,*
> *And often is his gold complexion dimmed;*
> *And every fair from fair sometime declines,*
> *By chance or nature's changing course untrimmed;*
> *But...*

[now to tom: with wonder]

> *...thy eternal summer shall not fade*
> *Nor lose possession of that fair thou ow'st;*
> *Nor shall Death brag thou wandrest in his shade,*
> *When in eternal lines to time thou grow'st...*

[18]

[tom interrupts]

tom   the words
               are you serious?
               have you
               listened

              to the words?

michael   i haven't entirely
              convinced you
              i take it

tom   you have
              you've convinced me that you don't practise what
              you preach

michael   i don't preach

tom   teach, then

michael   i don't teach either

tom   whatever the hell it is you do out front

michael   i put forward
              ideas

tom   can i put forward
              an idea:

michael

tom   say i'm henry

michael   henry?

tom   yes
              say i'm henry wriothesley
              and i'm sent:
              Look in thy glass, and tell the face thou viewest
              Now is the time that face should form another;
              Whose fresh repair if now thou not renewest,
              Thou dost beguile the world, unbless some mother,
              For where is she so fair whose uneared womb
              Disdains the tillage of thy husbandry?
              Or who is he so fond will be the tomb
              Of his self-love, to stop posterity?

michael   i am really familiar with it

tom   i know you're familiar with it
         but do you
         listen
         to it?

         Thou art thy mother's glass, and she in thee
         Calls back the lovely April of her prime:
         So thou through windows of thine age shalt see,
         Despite of wrinkles, this, thy golden time.
         *   But if thou live, remembered not to be,*
         *   Die single, and thine image dies with thee.*

                                                              [3]

henry   *'thy mother's glass'*
            my mother came to you for this?
            you've met
            my mother?

will   i haven't, no

henry   not my mother
            you haven't met my father, he is ten years dead

            not lord burghley
            surely
            this is not his style
            although it be his purpose
            nor sir thomas
            this is not sir thomas' purpose nor his care
            you've met

            hervey

            intrepid
            mister
            william
            hervey

            how much does he pay you?

will
            it is done in confidence

henry   how many of these doggerels am i to endure?

will   doggerels

henry *'So thou, thyself outgoing in thy noon,*
     unlooked on diest, unless thou get a son.'

                 [7]

will   well

henry i had you
     in the ascendant on london's firmament
     a jewel newly set within her crown
     i had you with the masters of your craft
     kit's match
     and far superior to nashe
     i laughed
     when greene disdained you
     laughed because i knew he's right to fear you
     i
     adored
     adonis

     my mother knows this and so hervey knows

     adonis was
     delectable
     it was
     inspired of you, you had me stomping round the
     house
     reciting
     living it
     of course i am adonis with their venuses they foist
     on me
     and it had
     everything:
     sensation
     spark
     desire
     lust
     if you'd had but a little patience
     i'd
     of course
     have been your patron based on
     venus and adonis

and your pieces at the theatre
i've seen them all, you must have had report
so
how could i refuse you, you
are possessed of
genius
but this

this

is an
insult
to civility:
'Is it for fear to wet a widow's eye
That thou consumest thyself in single life
Ah! if thou issueless shalt hap to die,
The world will wail thee, like a makeless wife'

[9]

well

not burghley
nor my mother
or
her ancient husband
whom i know, you know, he knows
she married merely for
his state alone, but
let alone her lover
hervey
and
least of all
a scribbling
sonneteer
though he be
shakespeare
tells
southampton
when to breed

[turns to leave]

will   sir

henry

will   i have
had report
that you have come to see my plays
frequently
repeatedly
it flattered, indeed
honoured me:
the young
earl of southampton

it's what
emboldened me
to dedicate my work to you

and
prompted by this dedication and your
known fondness
of my
words
as rightly you deduce
your mother's
friend
who holds her dear in his affection and seeks to
lift
what burdens weigh on her
besought me to
compose
for you some
well-intentioned
counsel

i see
now that i see you
face-to-face
not spy you from a distance or
behold a painter's so
inadequate
depiction of you
how
presumptuous
was my urging and how
most deficient
in describing you
my pen —

allow me
that i
beg
your pardon

henry

desist

parchment is dear
your
bought verse
renders it but
cheap

[an intense moment, a stand-off, almost, so to speak]

will   my verse is bought
            but not my eyes
            and not my ears
            and not my

henry

            not your?

will   no one truly
            ever
            buys
            a heart

henry   then let it never offered be
            for sale
            it is a precious heart that beats
            the passion of a poet
            such as you

will   you honour me to make me think so

henry   i honour those alone that i esteem
            and that alone was you
            until you so defiled yourself:
            'No love toward others in that bosom sits
            That on himself such murderous shame commits'

[9]

            'murderous shame'

has that not hervey writ all over it
are you so stooped to be my mother's and her
minion's
clerk?
does this hand of yours now
satisfy you
at the beck and call of their
dictation?

then shame on you: that is a sin more murderous
than any i with my hand
may
or may not
make myself
a guilty party to just as i please
at
will

will

[they hold each other's gaze again, none moves]

henry

will   and
you've come here
to tell me this?

henry

will   you are
quite certain that the purpose of your visit is my
admonishment
alone?

henry

will   an office that your footman could dispatch as easily
a messenger, a courier – by note, by letter, by
some
embassy

henry

will   yet you are here

henry

will   in person

henry

will   in my
            humble study and indeed
            abode

henry

will   on your own

henry

will

henry   and what
            pray
            make you of it?

will   of this i make that you are not in love
            nay
            cannot be

henry   i beg your pardon?

will   and surely will not
            ever
            neither

henry   how would you
            of all people –
            why am i not in love?
            i am as capable of love as any

will

            For shame deny that thou bearst love to any,
            Who for thyself art so unprovident.
            Grant, if thou wilt, thou art beloved of many,
            But that thou none lovest is most evident;

For thou art so possessed with murderous hate
That 'gainst thyself thou stickst not to conspire,
Seeking that beauteous roof to ruinate
Which to repair should be thy chief desire.
O, change thy thought, that I may change my mind!
Shall hate be fairer lodged than gentle love?
Be as thy presence is: gracious and kind,
Or to thyself at least kind-hearted prove:
    Make thee another self for love of me,
    That beauty still may live in thine or thee.

[10]

henry   'for love of me'?
            for love of

            thee

will

henry

[comes close to him; too close for mere comfort: there is a moment that could go either way; and as we switch time frames, the situation and therefore the tension is exactly the same]

tom

michael

[breaking the spell:]

michael   why henry
            why southampton?
            why not
            the earl of pembroke: william herbert
            there's plenty of evidence that points towards him
            and he's the son of will's employer after all
            lord pembroke:
            there's an obvious connection

tom   exactly

michael

tom   listen
to
the
words:

O that you were yourself, but love, you are
No longer yours than you yourself here live
Against this coming end you should prepare
And your sweet semblance to some other give...

michael i'm still really quite
conversant
with these sonnets

tom

...Dear my love, you know
You had a father: let your son say so.

[13]

michael

tom   had

had a father
lord pembroke
william herbert's father
is alive and kicking
he doesn't die until 1601
these are first mentioned in 1598
but now
if you allow now to be 1593
the theatres have been closed for half a year
because of the plague
will
aged twenty-nine
mostly unknown to the world outside his circle
needs money
needs a patron
and he needs things to happen in his life because
he's about to hit thirty and
as you yourself have pointed out
in london
in his day
you're doing well if you reach

                    thirty-five
michael   still: thirty is not old enough
                    to make his angst about his age seem
                    plausible

tom

                    how old are you?

michael

                    approaching fifty

tom   hah: case in point
                    you hesitate

michael   i didn't hesi

tom   you hesitate
                    you let a beat go by during which you process
                    you gauge
                    the implications of telling me your actual age
                    and then you say
                    'approaching fifty'
                    as if approaching fifty
                    was the same as
                    showing symptoms of syphilis
                    some sort of
                    disease
                    you don't say
                    i am fifty in june
                    with pride and joy and
                    confidence
                    because it scares you, you
                    think it makes you sound old
                    and you think you haven't achieved enough with
                    your life
                    and you think people don't fancy you if they know
                    your age
                    even though it's
                    obviously
                    on wikipedia and on your profile on the uni site:
                    anyone
                    who wants to know can know your age
                    so you are
                    exactly

as preoccupied with your age
at your age
as will is with his age
at his age
which
if you take away four hundred years of science
technology
medicine
and whatever we might call
civilisation
between him and you
is the precise same age as yours:
your approaching fifty
is the exact equivalent
to his approaching thirty
in fifteen ninety-four
which means we're now
in fifteen ninety-three
and not
as we would have to be
if i were
the earl of pembroke
in fifteen ninety-eight or sixteen hundred

michael

tom

michael   all right then
let's say
for the sake of argument
we're talking about
henry

what happens next?

tom   really?
coming from you?

look at you
the way you look at me
have done since i first set foot in one of your
lectures
you can't take your eyes off me

this
fascination
you have
with youth
with
'beauty'
you know it's in your eye and yet you treat it like an
absolute
because
you had it once and then you lost it? or
because you never had it?
or is this just something you do when you get old

michael   middle-aged

tom   to me: same difference
           remember: to you, when you were eighteen,
           nineteen, twenty-one?
           same difference

michael   how old are you?

tom   i'm twenty-two
           henry's nineteen
           and shakespeare
           at twenty-nine is having
           a midlife crisis

michael   yes i wouldn't put it like that, but

tom   just like you

michael   i wouldn't put this like that either, but

tom   if you're not having one now you will be by the time
           we start next term
           believe me, i've seen that look before: you're
           just about to buy yourself a menoporsch

michael

tom   either that
           or have an affair with one of your students

michael   i am, am i?

tom   it's
           on the cards

michael   and how
           do you think
           i should play them?

tom   affair first:
           time favours the sports car
           you can do that at seventy and more or less
           get away with it
           it'll seem less needy then than it does now – in fact:
           if you go for a nice vintage jag or similar
           then by the time you hit eighty
           you'll just about exude
           rogue style with it, which can
           all of its own be quite
           attractive

michael   you know a lot about
           rogue style
           for somebody your age

tom   i wonder why

michael

tom

michael   what's your name?

tom   tom

michael   hello tom

tom   hello
           michael

michael

           you see
           tom

william shakespeare
is in no position
to seduce
henry wriothesley
henry wriothesley is the ward of
lord burghley
lord burghley is lord high treasurer to the queen
possibly
the most powerful man
in the country

tom   no he is: he is
the most
powerful man in the country, but
will
does not
seduce
henry

michael

tom   remember:

michael

tom   henry
wriothesley
third
earl
of southampton
will not be
told
what to do
indeed
what
not
to do
by anyone

not by his mother
not by his mother's ancient husband
or by his mother's
young, attractive
lover

not even by
the queen
who
though she be nearing death
is quite
quite
taken with him
too, no
whatever

michael

henry what
ever
southampton does
he does
of
his own
volition

will

henry

michael

tom

2

at will's in london | lecture theatre
a few days later

henry   what's this?

will

henry   *'Not from the stars do I my judgment pluck;*
          And yet methinks I have astronomy'
          this is unsupportable
          'But from thine eyes my knowledge I derive'
          no methinks not
          'And, constant stars, in them I read such art
          As truth and beauty shall together thrive...'
          well how should that surprise me
          then
          words words words words words and then of course:
          Or else of thee this I prognosticate:
          Thy end is truth's and beauty's doom and date.'
                                                              [14]

will

henry   *'prognosticate?'*

          why
          do you
          persist?

will   three
          if not four
          found no favour with you
          at all
          i am commissioned to a dozen
          if i do not fulfil my commission to your
          satisfaction
          i may not claim the remainder of
          my fee

henry   you're not commissioned to satisfy me

you're commissioned to turn me into
a father

will   if i fail in the latter
i may be forgiven

to fail in the former
would be
inept

henry   tragic
more than inept
i warrant
but i
make no demand on you

will   yet you came back

again

henry   you wrote me another
and another
and *another*

will   and so they serve a purpose
after all

henry

will

henry   write me
another

will

henry

will   now?

henry   compose:
you are the poet
it is
surely

in your blood
your brain
your heart

go on

will

When I consider every thing that grows
Holds in perfection but a little moment,
That this huge stage presenteth nought but shows,
Whereon the stars in secret influence comment;
When I perceive that men as plants increase,
Cheerèd and checked e'en by the self-same sky,
Vaunt in their youthful sap, at height decrease,
And wear their brave state out of memory;
Then the conceit of this inconstant stay
Sets you most rich in youth before my sight,
Where wasteful Time debateth with Decay,
To change your day of youth to sullied night;
    And all in war with Time for love of you,
    As he takes from you, I engraft you new.

[15]

[a danger:]

henry   you
             engraft
             me

do you?

will

But wherefore do not you a mightier way
Make war upon this bloody tyrant, Time?
And fortify yourself in your decay
With means more blessèd than my barren rhyme?
Now stand you on the top of happy hours,
And many maiden gardens yet unset
With virtuous wish would bear your living flowers,
Much liker than your painted counterfeit:
So should the lines of life that life repair,
Which this, Time's pencil, or my pupil pen,

Neither in inward worth nor outward fair
Can make you live yourself in eyes of men.
To give away yourself keeps yourself still,
And you must live, drawn by your own sweet skill.

[16]

henry

well:
so i must
what though makes you think
i care
for maiden gardens

many or few

will   what any of us care for
any given time
may for that time become
our eden

henry   till we find
knowledge there

will   and then it's earthliness till heaven come

henry   or hell

will

[another intense moment pregnant with potential all way round]

tom

michael

tom   give me your mobile

i'll call you

michael   i'm away now for a few weeks

tom   off to?

michael   all over:

lecture tour

tom

why are you not
famous

michael   famous?

tom   talked about
recognised
bestseller kind of thing
signings at the bookstore
i don't agree with much of what you're saying
but
you do your work here, you travel around
your students appreciate you
i imagine your colleagues do
you're engaging
likeable
enough

michael

i'm not on TV

tom   is that the touchstone of quality?

michael   it's the touchstone
of fame but, you know:
Let those who are in favour with their stars
Of public honour and proud titles boast,
Whilst I, whom fortune of such triumph bars,
Unlooked for joy in that I honour most.

tom   *Great princes' favourites their fair leaves spread*
But as the marigold at the sun's eye,
And in themselves their pride lies burièd,
For at a frown they in their glory die.
The painful warrior famousèd for fight,
After a thousand victories once foiled,
Is from the book of honour razèd quite,
And all the rest forgot for which he toiled:

will   *Then happy I, that love and am beloved*
Where I may not remove nor be removed.

[25]

22

henry

will

henry   be not removed

will   i am
         obliged
         to the lord pembroke, he
         desires us
         his men
         to travel
         and perform
         some little plays
         i write for him

henry

         then go
         do as you please
         you say one thing and do another

         what are you to me?
         who are you
         to tell me
         what to do, where
         i may keep and whence remove you
         go
         do your service
         to some other master
         what do i care
         if you will stay or leave me
         you do presume
         too much
         for one so low
         go

will

henry   no: go

         i may not be a prince
         yet am i still
         the sovereign of my heart

and
i alone
say
when to see
if
to love
whether to even
think of
you

will

    i

shall
think of you and
i shall

write you

3

henry at his — will on tour
a couple of weeks or so later

[henry at the edge of the stage, sharing what he has received]

henry   *Lord of my love, to whom in vassalage*
Thy merit hath my duty strongly knit,
To thee I send this written ambassage,
To witness duty, not to show my wit:
Duty so great, which wit so poor as mine
May make seem bare, in wanting words to show it,
But that I hope some good conceit of thine
In thy soul's thought, all naked, will bestow it;
Till whatsoever star that guides my moving
Points on me graciously with fair aspect
And puts apparel on my tattered loving,
To show me worthy of thy sweet respect:
    Then may I dare to boast how I do love thee;
    Till then not show my head where thou mayst prove me.

[26]

is it a gift
to be loved
or is it a burden

i know it is
sweet pain
to ache for someone
one already owns

and own him quite
i do
his standing in the world is
nought, he ought
to me
be nothing

yet suddenly
i find without him

i no longer am
myself

am i too harsh on him?
he is
outrageous
insolent
obsessive
he is

sweet
and stubborn
and
and

he does with words
what no man does
with
any
thing

[will at a furthest possible distance]

will   *When, in disgrace with fortune and men's eyes,*
           I all alone beweep my outcast state
           And trouble deaf heaven with my bootless cries
           And look upon myself and curse my fate,
           Wishing me like to one more rich in hope,
           Featured like him, like him with friends possessed,
           Desiring this man's art and that man's scope,
           With what I most enjoy contented least;
           Yet in these thoughts, myself almost despising,
           Haply I think on thee, and then my state,
           Like to the lark at break of day arising
           From sullen earth, sings hymns at heaven's gate,
              For thy sweet love remembered such wealth brings
              That then I scorn to change my state with kings.

                                            [29]

4

a pub | a coffee house
a few weeks later: summer

tom   how was it?

michael   lonely, a bit, but
            a success

tom   it's good to see you
            extracurricularly
            as it were

michael   yes
            promise not to sue me for
            harassment

tom
            i have some excellent news

michael

tom   i was going to spend the rest of the summer with my
            family in the country
            we have a house

michael   when you say a house
            you mean

tom   an estate
            it's too big
            obviously, it's
            out of proportion
            it's preposterous really
            but

michael

tom   the good news is: my family won't be there
            so i'm inviting a few friends

                  join us
                  it'll be
                  fun

michael   fun?

tom   you do know what fun is
                  don't you
                  even at your age

michael
                  what would i be doing there

tom   spend time with me
                  go for walks
                  you could

                  write your book
                  that you keep talking about
                  but don't ever actually
                  seem to find the time to
                  work on

michael   it's an appealing thought

tom   it is

                  you'll have peace and quiet
                  and when you feel like it we can
                  talk poetry
                  debate
                  enjoy
                  elizabethan
                  dialectic

michael   with your friends

tom   oh they'll come and go
                  they're a laugh, they all
                  know about you anyway

michael   they do?

tom   i've read them some of your

	texts
michael	they're private
tom	i know but they're so sweet so honest
michael	aren't yours?
tom	yes but you wouldn't rate mine, would you they have no 'writerliness' about them do they?
michael	
tom	
michael	it's risky
tom	it's exciting
michael	in the current climate? i can lose my job, and you can you can be front page news i imagine
tom	come
	it'll do you good and otherwise we won't see each other for ages
michael	it would be nice to get out of town for a bit
henry	it will be safer too i cannot lose you to the plague, will

and is there aught for you to do
in london?

will   i can write while the theatre is closed

henry   then come to titchfield
write us a play for our
diversion

will   what about

henry   love

write us a play or two about love
love
and the labours of love: love's labours won and
love's labours lost

i will recompense you for your troubles and so
no question may arise why i delight in you
because
you will have work to do: at last
i'll be
your patron
too

5

at henry's titchfield estate
a few days later

[will and henry alone together, in privacy, with sensual joy and excitement]

will

henry

will   *Thy bosom is endearèd with all hearts*
              Which I, by lacking, have supposèd dead,
              And there reigns love and all love's loving parts,
              And all those friends which I thought burièd.
              How many a holy and obsequious tear
              Hath dear religious love stol'n from mine eye
              As interest of the dead, which now appear
              But things removed that hidden in thee lie!
              Thou art the grave where buried love doth live,
              Hung with the trophies of my lovers gone,
              Who all their parts of me to thee did give;
              That due of many now is thine alone:
                  Their images I loved I view in thee,
                  And thou, all they, hast all the all of me.

[31]

henry

will

henry

will

at tom's family's house | at henry's titchfield estate
a few days later

michael   friends
i heard you say 'friends'
i did not hear you say: 'with benefits'

tom   i'm sorry

michael   what
is that
about

tom   it's
i'm sorry
it isn't about anything, it's

stuff happens
doesn't it
it doesn't
mean
anything

he
doesn't mean

i
i was just
being stupid

sorry

michael   are you asserting your independence of me?
is that what that's about
in front of your friends?
is that
necessary?

why?

you invite me here, we have a
wonderful
wonderful
time together and
within a week
within a week
you

why?

will   *Why didst thou promise such a beauteous day,*
And make me travel forth without my cloak,
To let base clouds o'ertake me in my way,
Hiding thy bravery in their rotten smoke?
'Tis not enough that through the cloud thou break,
To dry the rain on my storm-beaten face,
For no man well of such a salve can speak
That heals the wound and cures not the disgrace:
Nor can thy shame give physic to my grief;
Though thou repent, yet I have still the loss:
Th' offender's sorrow lends but weak relief
To him that bears the strong offence's cross.

henry

will   *Ah! but those tears are pearl which thy love sheds,*
And they are rich and ransom all ill deeds.

[34]

henry   i do
beg
your
forgiveness
i am
incapable
it seems
of love
am
destined
it is plain to me
to
be
forever
an offence

33

in all men's eyes
and now
in thine?
have i
too much
to value what i have, to ever
ever
cherish it?

will

henry

will

no henry
no
No more be grieved at that which thou hast done:
Roses have thorns, and silver fountains mud,
Clouds and eclipses stain both moon and sun,
And loathsome canker lives in sweetest bud.
All men make faults, and even I in this,
Authorising thy trespass with compare,
Myself corrupting, salving thy amiss,
Excusing thy sins more than thy sins are;
For to thy sensual fault I bring in sense –
Thy adverse party is thy advocate –
And 'gainst myself a lawful plea commence.
Such civil war is in my love and hate
    That I an accessary needs must be
      To that sweet thief which sourly robs from me.

[35]

**at henry's titchfield estate | at tom's family's house —
michael at home**
the next day

[henry alone, reading]

henry   *Let me confess that we two must be twain,*
Although our undivided loves are one:
So shall those blots that do with me remain
Without thy help by me be borne alone.
In our two loves there is but one respect,
Though in our lives a separable spite,
Which though it alter not love's sole effect,
Yet doth it steal sweet hours from love's delight.
I may not evermore acknowledge thee,
Lest my bewailed guilt should do thee shame,
Nor thou with public kindness honour me,
Unless thou take that honour from thy name:
     But do not so; I love thee in such sort
     As, thou being mine, mine is thy good report.

[36]

*[**tom** on the phone to michael]*

tom   and what is *that* about?
you say you can't be angry with me and then
you
disappear

michael   your friends are making fun of you
they're certainly making fun of me
but i don't even mind that
i know
i am
ridiculous
as your
'boyfrlend'
but you

you're always

only
a long lens away from a
story
because of who you are

i
don't want to drag you into this
i don't want to drag you into
anything
it would be
irresponsible
of me to do so

tom you're afraid of my
    friends?
    i know they're obnoxious
    some of them, but

michael i'm not afraid, i
    i
    just don't want to be
    a liability
    and no
    i don't entirely trust them
    nor
    in all likelihood
    should you
    certainly not all of them
    there are some people there
    around you who

tom
    go on

michael whom i think you should be
    wary
    of

tom what's brought this on?

michael you notice, you
    overhear
    things
    chatter

tom so what?
   they are idiots, by and large
   compared to you they are
   illiterate
   who cares what
   any of them
   think?

michael

tom come back

michael i can't

   i have
   accepted an offer
   of a stint abroad
   i'm teaching a course

tom how long

michael one term
   till the end of the year

tom call me

michael i will

tom please
   don't text me
   call me

michael i will

tom please?

henry at home in london — will on tour | tom at home
a few weeks later

[henry, writing – will reading]

henry   and so this
with
remorse
and sadness
i confess

i miss you, will

these lonely, long months
from your side

i
miss
you, will
and
missing you i
churlishly
nay wantonly
took that which wasn't mine to take

i
yet again
ask
your forgiveness
though
i fear
we may not now
be reconciled
but
if it were to serve thee to absolve me:
she too, too soon
too willingly
gave in to me
and
thinking her yours, i

bethought you
through her
mine

[will directly to henry, as if they were in the same room together:]

will   *Take all my loves, my love, yea, take them all;*
What hast thou then more than thou hadst before?
No love, my love, that thou mayst true love call;
All mine was thine before thou hadst this more.
Then if for my love thou my love receivest,
I cannot blame thee for my love thou usest;
But yet be blamed, if thou thyself deceivest
By wilful taste of what thyself refusest.
I do forgive thy robbery, gentle thief,
Although thou steal thee all my poverty;
And yet, love knows, it is a greater grief
To bear love's wrong than hate's known injury.
     Lascivious grace, in whom all ill well shows,
     Kill me with spites; yet we must not be foes.

[40]

*[**tom** on the phone]*

tom   yeah mate i know
hyah, let's

no, he's away for another couple of months

i try, but
you know
it's
i get horny, i get
no it's true i get
lonely
i actually genuinely miss him
i actually genuinely

yes
yes i do

no of course i haven't told him that

well

well because
you don't tell someone you love them until

too late?
no
no it isn't
it's not too late, is it?
why
would it be too late?

yes i know

yes i know
no i will
yes

well
at least i'm not getting off with the woman he's
having an affair with

no he isn't having an affair
not that i'm aware of anyway

no i wouldn't be getting off with her if he did
it's
it's like a reference
oh never mind

it's
you know on facebook
when people used to put
"it's complicated?"
well
that's what it is
it's

complicated

9

at henry's in london
st nicholas day

[henry and will, together again]

will

henry

will   i brought you
            a gift
            for st nicholas

henry

will

henry   you had time to write?

will   i had time to think of you and when
            thinking of you
            while being from you
            filled me with sorrow
            i
            made time
            to write for you

henry
            the rape of lucrece

will   i had inscribed *adonis* with a promise

henry   so you had
            you promised me a
            'graver labour'

will   and i fear it is

henry   *"The love I dedicate to your Lordship is without end*
            what I have done is yours

what I have to do is yours
being part in all I have
devoted yours"

i do know how to thank you
will
i know just how to reward and thank you

come

will

henry

will

henry

will   *So am I as the rich, whose blessèd key*
Can bring him to his sweet up-lockèd treasure,
The which he will not every hour survey,
For blunting the fine point of seldom pleasure.

henry *Therefore are feasts so solemn and so rare,*
Since, seldom coming, in the long year set,
Like stones of worth they thinly placèd are,
Or captain jewels in the carcanet.

will   *So is the time that keeps you as my chest,*
Or as the wardrobe which the robe doth hide,
To make some special instant special blest,
By new unfolding his imprison'd pride.
  Blessèd are you, whose worthiness gives scope,
  Being had, to triumph, being lacked, to hope.

[52]

10

at henry's in london | at tom's
the following day

[in the soft morning, henry asleep]

will   *What is your substance, whereof are you made,*
          That millions of strange shadows on you tend?
          Since every one hath, every one, one shade,
          And you, but one, can every shadow lend.
          Describe Adonis, and the counterfeit
          Is poorly imitated after you;
          On Helen's cheek all art of beauty set,
          And you in Grecian tires are painted new:
          Speak of the spring and foison of the year;
          The one doth shadow of your beauty show,
          The other as your bounty doth appear;
          And you in every blessèd shape we know.
               In all external grace you have some part,
               But you like none, none you, for constant heart.

[53]

*[will gets up, leaves – **tom** wakes, discovers and reads]*

tom   *Being your slave, what should I do but tend*
          Upon the hours and times of your desire?
          I have no precious time at all to spend,
          Nor services to do, till you require.
          Nor dare I chide the world-without-end hour
          Whilst I, my sov'reign, watch the clock for you,
          Nor think the bitterness of absence sour
          When you have bid your servant once adieu;
          Nor dare I question with my jealous thought
          Where you may be, or your affairs suppose,
          But, like a sad slave, stay and think of nought
          Save, where you are how happy you make those.
               So true a fool is love that in your will,
               Though you do any thing, he thinks no ill.

[57]

*[**michael** returns]*

michael

tom   you all right?

michael   do you have
           a girlfriend?

tom   sorry?

michael   would you feel
           able
           to have a girlfriend

tom   i've got a pretty busy week ahead

michael   if you wanted to
           or a boyfriend
           for that matter

tom   and next week too
           as it happens

michael   apart from me
           obviously
           but you see i'm not even sure that i
           count as your
           'boyfriend'
           for any number of reasons
           the obvious one being in the
           terminology

           strange that
           isn't it

tom   what is

michael   we're finally free
           to be free of a label
           and yet
           there is this
           need
           to brand ourselves

                        still

tom   we can meet up
               the weekend?

michael   and then always
               this nagging feeling that
               if things are going well
               if things are going
               swimmingly
               there must be
               something
               wrong

tom   i'm going to get some milk
               do you want anything

*[tom gets up to leave; michael faces himself in a mirror or on a
screen; tom, not actually having left, watches. exactly the same for
henry and **will**]*

will   *Sin of self-love possesseth all mine eye
               And all my soul and all my every part;
               And for this sin there is no remedy,
               It is so grounded inward in my heart.
               Methinks no face so gracious is as mine,
               No shape so true, no truth of such account;
               And for myself mine own worth do define,
               As I all other in all worths surmount.
               But when my glass shows me myself indeed,
               Beated and chopped with tanned antiquity,
               Mine own self-love quite contrary I read;
               Self so self-loving were iniquity.
                   'Tis thee, myself, that for myself I praise,
                   Painting my age with beauty of thy days.*

                                                              [62]

[henry takes will by the hand, engages him in a slow dance]

henry   *When I have seen by Time's fell hand defaced
               The rich proud cost of outworn buried age;
               When sometime lofty towers I see down-razed
               And brass eternal slave to mortal rage;
               When I have seen the hungry ocean gain*

Advantage on the kingdom of the shore,
And the firm soil win of the watery main,
Increasing store with loss and loss with store;
When I have seen such interchange of state,
Or state itself confounded to decay;
Ruin hath taught me thus to ruminate,
That Time will come and take my love away.
This thought is as a death, which cannot choose
But weep to have that which it fears to lose.

[64]

think not on time
think not on me
think not on death
not for a while

death will come
i'll be hence
time passes every moment that you breathe
so
live
my friend
and let me live
a while
with thee

will

henry

11

at tom's | at henry's in london
a couple of months later: february 94

tom   sup?

michael   at your age
            tell me because i can't remember
            do you ever get to the point where you are simply
            fed up

tom

michael   with everything

tom

michael   because at my age i can tell you
            you do

tom   what happened

michael   does it matter?
            when everything always happens
            in exactly the same way

tom

michael   the publisher
            on the point of signing a deal
            for the book
            through the new agent
            decides that
            i am too much of a risk
            'in this difficult climate'
            why?
            they say: because there is such a
            limited market
            they mean:
            because i'm proposing
            one chapter

that is
politically contentious

tom   you mean incorrect

michael   there is no correctness in politics
there are
opinions
and there are
facts
facts you have to take in their context and mostly
with a pinch of salt

opinions
you can argue over
in fact you have to
that's what they're for
otherwise they wouldn't be opinions
they would be facts
but that's all
by the by

tom   is there such a thing as
fact though?

michael   well exactly
that's also a matter of
opinion
but not in the way it's being twisted
right out of sense
right now: is there such a thing as fact
within our frame of reference and reality?
absolutely
could it be that our frame of reference and therefore
our reality
is simply not yet fully understood
and our facts are therefore
at some point going to turn out
to have been a fiction?
absolutely it could be: we know
because we've been there before
does that mean
that fact and fiction, let alone
fantasy

all are the same
absolutely not
how
can this be so difficult
to grasp?

tom

michael

tom   this is not what your chapter is about

michael   no this is in answer to your question
            is there such a thing as fact?

tom   what's your chapter about

michael   the dark lady

tom

michael   it is obvious to me
            as you know
            that the dark lady appears in the relationship
            between shakespeare and wriothesley
            (assuming for the sake of argument it is wriothesley)

tom   you're coming around to this!…

michael   i'm allowing for the possibility

            that the dark lady appears in the relationship
            between shakespeare and wriothesley
            if it is wriothesley
            long before she appears in the canon

tom   how is this controversial

michael   it isn't very

tom   then what is

michael   i contend that her impact on shakespeare
            notwithstanding

and in fact on the young man
with both of whom she is having an affair
is nowhere near as emotionally encompassing
and therefore draining
and therefore also fulfilling
and therefore
relevant
as
and thus on a par with
that of the fair youth

tom   how can you say *such a thing?*

michael   more or less my publisher's words

tom   but that's not all

michael   of course that's not all:
nobody
least of all i
would deny that the dark lady is a fascinating
character
who merits
study and a great deal of
attention
and who
upends
shakespeare's emotional world
in a way few people do
that is not
in question

tom

michael   the chapter puts this in a larger context that
examines
will's relationship with women, social class, and
therefore
status
generally

tom   ouch

michael   exactly: and as a supposedly straight male

remember i am still officially supposedly straight
i am here entering
dodgy territory, or
as my publisher puts it
skating on
thin ice

tom   obviously

michael   and so
because of this
because i am not allowed
apparently
to give my take on a constellation that lies
four hundred years in the past, remember,
and that doesn't fit
our current contemporary perception of gender
gender roles and
equality
we now
have no book

tom   if it's one chapter
why don't you just
take it out?

michael   because that's what civilised endeavour is about
argument and counter-argument
disputation
how
can you have
culture
when at the slightest whiff of disagreement you go
not for
discourse
but
conformity?

henry   indeed
but why such
anguish
over what
the world
opines?

why
credit
their censure
with
import?

will   because an honest heart
craves justice, needs
the world it beats in
to be
fair
deserves
for its invention
recompense

yet all about
injustices
prevail; unfairness is the rule and
i
and i am not alone in this i know
am kept
invisible in
shadows, and

i am tired
henry
and
Tired with all these, for restful death I cry,
As, to behold desert a beggar born,
And needy nothing trimmed in jollity,
And purest faith unhappily forsworn,
And guilded honour shamefully misplaced,
And maiden virtue rudely strumpeted,
And right perfection wrongfully disgraced,
And strength by limping sway disablèd,
And art made tongue-tied by authority,
And folly doctor-like controlling skill,
And simple truth miscalled simplicity,
And captive good attending captain ill:
    Tired with all these, from these would I be gone,
    Save that, to die, I leave my love alone.

[66]

12

on neutral ground in the open
a few months later: summer

henry   the sun is restored onto your face

will   and for good reason

henry

will   we are to become the lord chamberlain's men

henry   my lord hunsdon?

will   has graced us with his
            favour

henry   how so?

will   the lady vernon spoke on our behalf

henry   how most
            convenient

will   quite so

henry   i know the lady vernon well

will   i know
            and yet
            i know i know her better

henry

will   before i knew you
            some two, three years since

henry   the lady vernon
            is lady-in-waiting to the queen

will   and has been

for some time

henry how
do you know her

will henry
we regularly perform at court

whenever
the queen is in attendance
the lady vernon
waits
on her

these
long
hours of
waiting
an actor whose part is none too large
(though yet his part be none too small)
may
quicken
for her
if she so
desires

henry *confound* me
lady vernon

will

henry she's no beauty

will no
her
chief attraction
is not
the aspect
of her head

henry *confound* me

lady
vernon

13

at michael's | at will's in london
a couple of months later: september

tom   have you seen this?

michael

           that's pure tabloid pap

tom   it's
           unwelcome

michael   i know

           i'm sorry
           i'm sorry they do this to you
           all of you actually
           and i'm
           really sorry
           i seem to be the cause of it

tom   i
           i wouldn't care if it were just about me, but
           it's always
           about my mother
           about my mother's boyfriend
           about my dad
           even though he hasn't been around in years
           i

           we really don't need this at the moment
           my family: we're
           we're under
           constant scrutiny
           everything matters, every
           move
           can be construed as false
           and normally is, i

           i don't know what to do

i don't know how to deal with it

how do i deal with this?

how? how does
anybody
deal with this

michael   shhh

don't
just
don't

don't try to
deal with it, let it
wash
over you

henry   wash over me?
it goes too far, it
probes too deep
it reaches to the core and it will cause alarm
where no alarm may
ever
sound:
*"there is some thing under these false names and
showes
that hath been done truly"*
how does he know
and who
who is this
willobie?

will

henry   *"alway
alway the same"*
you know the meaning of this
do you not?

this willobie
(scribbler, pamphleteer
whoever he may be)

in his small tale
that he's made up and yet of which he says
there is the grain of truth in it
(though grains of truth may yield
a field of
slander)
has an
h.w.
(clearly me)
who not long ago shared with his
"familiar friend"
w.s.
(clearly you)
"the curtesy" of a
"like passion"
(a wench we both remember all too well)
resulting in a
"like infection"
(i scarcely need remind us)
court
a lady named
avisa
who
rejects his advances
in letters signed
"always the same"
semper eadem: always the same

semper eadem
is the motto
of our queen
he puts it about
that i
of all people
have designs
on
our queen, will
our
queen

will willobie
    may not mean the
    queen

henry   who does he mean?

will   he may mean
the lady vernon
our
lady-in-waiting
to the queen

henry

will   whom as you know
i know
as well if not
at least as yet
a little better still
than
you

henry

will   but
yes
whomsoever he may mean
and whatsoever be the cause that he
may
or
may not
have
for doing so
he
surely
surely
is here playing with some
fire

henry   and we
are perched on the barrel
that has
gunpowder
in it

will

henry

will   *That thou art blamed shall not be thy defect,*
For slander's mark was ever yet the fair;
The ornament of beauty is suspect,
A crow that flies in heaven's sweetest air.
So thou be good, slander doth but approve
Thy worth the greater, being wooed of time;
For canker vice the sweetest buds doth love,
And thou present'st a pure unstainèd prime.
Thou hast passed by the ambush of young days,
Either not assailed or victor being charged;
Yet this thy praise cannot be so thy praise,
To tie up envy evermore enlarged:
If some suspect of ill masked not thy show,
Then thou alone kingdoms of hearts shouldst owe.

[70]

tom   i don't
want to
have to
deal with this
kind of thing
any more

michael   i know

i know, and
i know what i need to do
i'm afraid

i know
too well
what i need to do

tom

michael

14

at henry's in london | at tom's
a day or two later

[tom on his own; receives a text, then another, and another; and another couple more. reads:]

tom   *No longer mourn for me when I am dead*
Then you shall hear the surly sullen bell
Give warning to the world that I am fled
From this vile world
                with vilest worms to dwell:
Nay, if you read this line, remember not
The hand that writ it; for I love you so
That I in your sweet thoughts
                would be forgot
If thinking on me then should make you woe.
O, if, I say, you look upon this verse
When I perhaps compounded am with clay,

Do not so much as my poor name rehearse.
But let your love e'en with my life decay,
   Lest the wise world should look into your moan

   And mock you with me after I am gone.

                                          [71]

[tom dials, waits, listens, speaks]

tom   i'm coming over

          right now

15

at michael's
less than an hour later

tom   what do you think you're doing?

michael

tom   you scared me

michael

tom   don't
             ever
             do this to me again

michael

tom   you don't send me morose messages
             that make me think you're about to top yourself

michael

tom   and you don't mope around here
             pitying yourself: you have
             work to do

michael

tom   write
             the book
             and put in it everything you want to say
             regardless
             claim
             your
             place in the world
             now

michael

             i don't think you should come here

at least not
till this has all
blown over

tom   i'm not the person to let
anyone
tell me
who i can see
how
when
or where —
you should know me better than that

michael   i'm not your vent
i'm not your vent to
get back
at people
to
assert your
independence and
show them how
free
you are
there's

too much
at stake
there's more
at stake
at any rate
than that

tom   it's not about them

maybe it once was
but it isn't now

not any more

michael   are you sure?

tom

michael

henry

will

henry   don't doubt me
will
yes
there are
powers
greater than mine
i know
and they want things
for me
and for themselves
i do not care for
and they may yet
prevail
but even if they do
don't doubt me
and don't doubt

i love you

will

henry

will   *That time of year thou mayst in me behold*
When yellow leaves, or none, or few, do hang
Upon those boughs which shake against the cold,
Bare ruined choirs, where late the sweet birds sang.
In me thou seest the twilight of such day
As after sunset fadeth in the west,
Which by and by black night doth take away,
Death's second self, that seals up all in rest.
In me thou seest the glowing of such fire
That on the ashes of his youth doth lie,
As the death-bed whereon it must expire
Consumed with that which it was nourished by.
    This thou perceivest, which makes thy love more strong,
    To love that well which thou must leave ere long.

[73]

16

at will's in london | at michael's
a few weeks later: late october

will   what news

henry   i am a free man

will   when were you ever not a free man
            henry

henry   when i was
            shackled
            to the prospect
            of an ill-matched
            marriage

will   what have you done
            henry?

henry   i have
            unshackled
            myself

will   henry
            what
            have
            you
            done?

henry   i have paid off the lady vere

will   you have done
            what?

henry   the lady vere
            that everyone has been so keen for me to marry
            that you yourself have given yourself over to
            importune me to bed and wed and
            impregnate
            so she spit forth a brat

well
you were right
but not when you were doing hervey's bidding, you
were right in saying
that when i stole your mistress
it was
wilful taste
of what i normally refuse

it was
wilful
and it was wrong
i enjoyed her only
for being
yours

why then
would i keep this
dread
about me
of the lady vere

will   henry:
what
have you
done?

henry   i paid her the ransom of five thousand pounds

tom   *five thousands pounds?*
that's like
what
in today's money
that's

michael   two and a half, three million
thereabouts?

tom   to
not
marry someone

michael   he
doesn't want to get hitched to that girl

tom   he really doesn't
           and she's the queen's lady-in-waiting

michael   no that's lady vernon
           this is lady vere
           granddaughter to none other than
           lord burghley
           who you remember is
           henry's guardian and effectively
           adoptive father

tom   he is paying
           the granddaughter of his adoptive father

michael   effectively, not
           technically

tom   effectively adoptive father
           who technically is the most powerful man in the
           country

michael   effectively too

tom   henry's paying his granddaughter
           five grand
           not
           to marry her

michael   is the long and the short of it

tom   he really doesn't want to get hitched
           to that girl
           or any girl, it seems

michael   no
           he really doesn't
           though he does so later
           to the lady vernon
           not the lady vere

tom

michael

tom then what's all this about?

michael proving something to will?
proving something to burghley?
to his mother?
his mother's
earnest and
very young
lover?

maybe just to himself, maybe
he just needs to
prove something
to himself

or
he clings on to the bit of freedom he has for as long
as he can
like any young man
before
ultimately
he succumbs
to the convention
of his age
like most of us
eventually
do

tom we do, do we?
you don't

michael

no
i don't
maybe i have that
one thing
in my
favour

tom

it is not the only thing
michael

michael what really intrigues me is this:

say
you were my patron
as opposed to
whatever it is we would call each other now
say you're my patron and
you've had this willobie story break on you:
you know you should lie low and
distance yourself from me in public
not because you want to but
because you have to

say
the monarchy, the
nation
your livelihood, in fact
your life
may well depend on it

tom

michael   why
at that precise moment
would you not only
spectacularly
break off a long-arranged marriage
at incredible expense
but on top of that
take on
another poet?

tom   i do, do i?

michael   you do

tom   at this precise moment
i become
patron
to another poet?

michael

by the sounds of it:
Whilst I alone did call upon thy aid,
My verse alone had all thy gentle grace,
But now my gracious numbers are decayed

And my sick Muse doth give another place.
I grant, sweet love, thy lovely argument
Deserves the travail of a worthier pen…

[79]

tom   have a look?

michael

tom   that is really simple

michael   oh i'm glad
i thought it was
complicated

tom   what are we now?
autumn ninety-four?
you have a scandal breaking
people satirise you
this willobie character is
implicating
the queen herself
or if not her
then at any rate
her lady-in-waiting
who just happens to be
an old flame of your lover's
whom you yourself may
already have your eyes on
in view of what you've just told me
all of which
is just
asking for trouble
of the highest order
somebody – and whether it's just
willobie
or whether there is somebody else, somebody
more
powerful
behind him –
somebody
no matter who
is stirring things up
pretty deliberately

trying to get
henry
and his
special
slightly
older friend
will
noticed, maybe
exposed

so if i'm henry wriothesley
put yourself in my shoes:
you are
the ward of burghley
most powerful man in the country
you are
effectively a godson to the queen
if not in name then almost certainly in
constellation

a bit over a year ago you were called
by none other than nashe
then top of the pile as far as writers are concerned
"a dear lover and cherisher
as well of the lovers of poets, as of poets themselves"
and clearly you are
in fact
for the last eighteen months you've been a
dear lover
of one poet in particular

what do you do?
you either
cut off the poets altogether and say: no more poets
no more a lover of any of them
or you say
what's wrong with loving poets
i love their work their minds their words
i am
a dear lover of poets, that's what i am
and he
well he's just
one of them

you deflect
attention
so you don't have to
deflect
your poet

michael

will doesn't quite get that

tom   *O, how I faint when I of you do write,*
Knowing a better sp'rit doth use your name,
And in the praise thereof spends all his might,
To make me tongue-tied, speaking of your fame!
But since your worth, wide as the ocean is,
The humble as the proudest sail doth bear,
My saucy bark inferior far to his
On your broad main doth wilfully appear.
Your shallowest help will hold me up afloat,
Whilst he upon your soundless deep doth ride;
Or being wrecked, I am a worthless boat,
He of tall building and of goodly pride:
    Then if he thrive and I be cast away,
    The worst was this; my love was my decay.

[80]

no
will doesn't get that
he thinks he's cloying him
and maybe
he is

although to be frank
by the sounds of this
he's got reason to be jealous
on account of more than just
the potency of this
rival poet's
words

michael   maybe he is cloying him
or maybe
life is

at henry's in london
a few months later: early 95

henry i am
    will
    at a loss

    i want you near me, will, i
    relish you

    i know i
    betray you, i
    injure you without
    meaning to and sometimes
    i may even
    mean to
    without knowing why

    i am
    incapable of being
    what the world expects of me
    i'm weak
    when those around me deem me strong

    but now
    i am in grave
    grave
    danger
    will

    i felt
    one time
    that i was
    unassailable
    earl of southampton
    a favourite at court

    you know i
    jousted once before the queen
    and she commended me

but the queen loves me not
she fears me
as she would fear you
if you were dangerous
but you
will
are a lamb
and you must not be slaughtered

ram up will
and become
a man your kingdom's tongue will praise

i will
betray you
yet again
i will
be frowned upon and
mocked
that is my part
on this grand stage of ours
but you and i know this
(perhaps one day the world will know)
that we were once as one:
what men are putting now asunder
had once
the blessing of the sun

will
     you are preparing
     to leave me?

henry   i am not preparing, will
     i am forestalling
     that which i most dread

at will's in london
a few weeks later

will   the lady vernon?

henry   i fear so

will   lady vernon?

henry   aye

will   but henry
of all the women in the world the
lady vernon

henry   that chief attraction of hers that you
praised
is
unimpeachable

will   *but you are not*
why
go after
lady vernon

henry   i went not after her, she
came for me

will   why not say no?
why
risk
incensing so the queen
why
stab me in the heart
by taking
her

henry   i could not
refuse
the lady vernon

refusing her would be refusing you
if to be with her is to make her glad
then her being yours and i being hers
most gladdest will be
you

will   for heaven's sake
do you
ever
hear yourself?

How sweet and lovely dost thou make the shame
Which, like a canker in the fragrant rose,
Doth spot the beauty of thy budding name!
O, in what sweets dost thou thy sins enclose!
That tongue that tells the story of thy days,
Making lascivious comments on thy sport,
Cannot dispraise but in a kind of praise;
Naming thy name blesses an ill report.
O, what a mansion have those vices got
Which for their habitation chose out thee,
Where beauty's veil doth cover every blot,
And all things turn to fair that eyes can see!
    Take heed, dear heart, of this large privilege;
    The hardest knife ill-used doth lose his edge.

[95]

henry   no will, no
don't hate me, will
no matter what i do

i
have
nothing
i am
nobody

do you think
i want this for myself:
a life prescribed by
marriage, children, death?
you yourself have it at home
your little hamnet and the girls
a doting woman who looks after them

is it for you?
is it enough?
is it your paradise?
then why this eden of our own
what have we not
when we do have each other

but
i am
well of age, i am
responsible for an estate, i
have a name to propagate
and
yes
i am
already old
worn out
by these demands on me
knowing
that no matter how i play my cards
up comes the queen
and i defer to her
i'm tired to my death, will
and i despair that to my death
i may not walk
with you

will   oh henry

To me, fair friend, you never can be old,
For as you were when first your eye I eyed,
Such seems your beauty still. Three winters cold
Have from the forests shook three summers' pride,
Three beauteous springs to yellow autumn turned
In process of the seasons have I seen,
Three April perfumes in three hot Junes burned,
Since first I saw you fresh, which yet are green.
Ah, yet doth beauty, like a dial-hand,
Steal from his figure and no pace perceived;
So your sweet hue, which methinks still doth stand,
Hath motion and mine eye may be deceived:
For fear of which, hear this, thou age unbred;
Ere you were born was beauty's summer dead.

[104]

and as for me?

Alas, 'tis true I have gone here and there
And made myself a motley to the view,
Gored mine own thoughts, sold cheap what is most dear,
Made old offences of affections new;
Most true it is that I have looked on truth
Askance and strangely: but, by all above,
These blenches gave my heart another youth,
And worse essays proved thee my best of love.
Now all is done, have what shall have no end:
Mine appetite I never more will grind
On newer proof, to try an older friend,
A god in love, to whom I am confined.
    Then give me welcome, next my hea'en the best,
    E'en to thy pure and most most loving breast.

[110]

19

at tom's | at henry's in london
a year later: summer 96

michael   it's done

tom

michael   they've signed
          we'll publish
          in the spring

tom   congratulations

michael   i'm dedicating it to you

tom   why?

michael   you
          put me on to this, you
          made me do it

tom   all right
          i was your catalyst

michael   that sounds so
          utilitarian

tom   muse?

michael   that would be flattery

tom   inspiration

michael   therapy
          maybe you've been my
          therapy

          will that do?

tom   i'm glad i was of help

michael   you were
thank you, you
are
you are
of help

tom

michael   i don't know what to make of you
i don't know what to make of us
but

tom   who does?
no point
questioning it
just
go with it
surrender control
it will take us exactly where it needs to go
where we need to go
just
trust it
it's
easy
really

michael   too easy
maybe?

tom   michael
listen
just
listen
to the words
if you listen to the words
you'll know what this is
even if it doesn't
cannot
last

what matter
listen
to the words:

Let me not to the marriage of true minds
Admit impediments. Love is not love
Which alters when it alteration finds,
Or bends with the remover to remove:
O no! it is an ever-fixèd mark
That looks on tempests and is never shaken;
It is the star to every wandering bark,
Whose worth's unknown, although his height be taken.
Love's not Time's fool, though rosy lips and cheeks
Within his bending sickle's compass come:
Love alters not with his brief hours and weeks,
But bears it out e'en to the edge of doom.

will   *If this be error and upon me proved,*
             I never writ, nor no man ever loved.

[116]

henry

on unknown ground
soon after: august

henry

will

henry   i know not what to say will

will

henry   words
can no more heal the wound
his absence carves
into your heart
than call him back

will

henry   may god
make heaven welcome him
your poor boy
your

poor hamnet

poor
sweet
hamnet

god rest his darling soul

will

henry

will

henry   write them
plays

       will, write
       another
       and another
       and another still

       write your pain into your plays
       and make their hearts soar
       write them
       hearts
       that deep within know
       everything
       all that you've loved
       all that you've lost
       all that you've lived
       and they will
       know you
       as they know
       themselves

will

henry

[henry lies; will cradles, then lets go of him]

will   *O thou, my lovely boy, who in thy power*
              Dost hold Time's fickle glass, his sickle, hour;
              Who hast by waning grown, and therein show'st
              Thy lovers withering as thy sweet self grow'st;
              If Nature, sovereign mistress over wrack,
              As thou goest onwards, still will pluck thee back,
              She keeps thee to this purpose, that her skill
              May time disgrace and wretched minutes kill.
              Yet fear her, O thou minion of her pleasure!
              She may detain, but not still keep, her treasure:
              Her audit, though delayed, answered must be,
              And her quietus is to render thee.
                 (   )
                 (   )

                                                   [126]

[tom still lies, then michael kisses his head, makes to leave; turns]

21

lecture theatre
now

[michael continuing where he left off:]

michael
> *So long as men can breathe or eyes can see*
> *So long lives this, and this gives life to thee.*

[18]

end

A Note on the Text

Incorporating sonnets by William Shakespeare in this play, I obviously had to make some editorial decisions, not only as to which ones to choose and whether to use a sonnet in full or in parts, but also about how to render them on the page.

In doing so, I mostly referred – and gladly deferred – to established scholarly editions, namely the New Penguin edition of *The Sonnets and A Lover's Complaint,* edited by John Kerrigan, and The Oxford Shakespeare edition of *The Complete Sonnets and Poems,* edited by Stanley Wells.

Bearing in mind, however, that this is a play and therefore the main purpose of the sonnets here is for them to be spoken as part of a dialogue, I have aligned and standardised spellings foremost with clarity for the actor in mind.

Specifically:

- In line with common practice, past tense endings which a contemporary English speaker would not pronounce as a syllable are marked with an accent where required for prosody. *[burièd]*

- Where meaning and rhythm remain unaffected by doing so, archaic spellings have been contemporised. For instance, Wells has *rememb'red not to be* in Sonnet 3, line 11, whereas Kerrigan has *remembered.* In cases like this, I have followed Kerrigan's example.

- Most editors do not specifically mark instances where words like *heaven* or *even* are pronounced as one syllable. To aid the actor, I have done so where relevant. *[hea'en, e'en]*

Generally, I have favoured leaving sonnets intact, as the idea and really the point of the play is to treat them as fully integral to the text. I am conscious, of course, that they were not written as dialogue and that this, therefore, constitutes an artifice to support a story that may or may not have happened as represented here. That is the conceit of this play.

Everything *is* conjecture. Except the words.

Sebastian Michael
London, August 2022